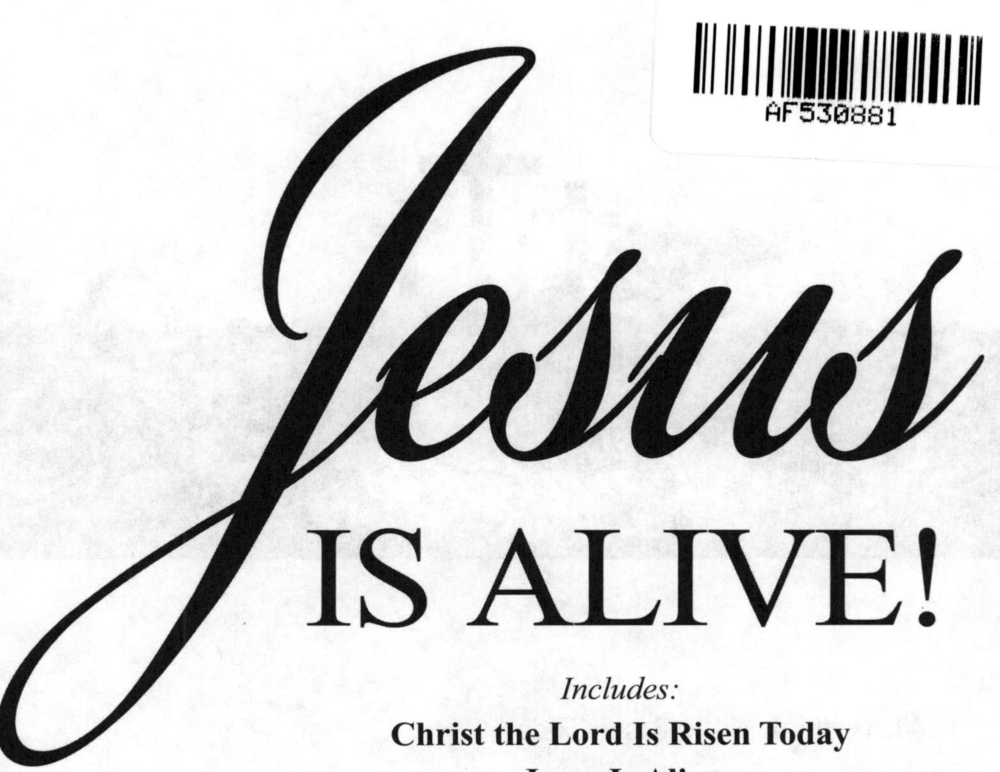

Includes:

Christ the Lord Is Risen Today

Jesus Is Alive

All to Us

Jesus Saves

An Easter Worship Service Package

Arranged & Orchestrated by

Daniel Semsen

lillenas.com

Contents

Christ the Lord Is Risen Today

CHARLES WESLEY, DANIEL SEMSEN
and CHRISTY SEMSEN

Lyra Davidica, DANIEL SEMSEN
and CHRISTY SEMSEN
Arr. by Daniel Semsen

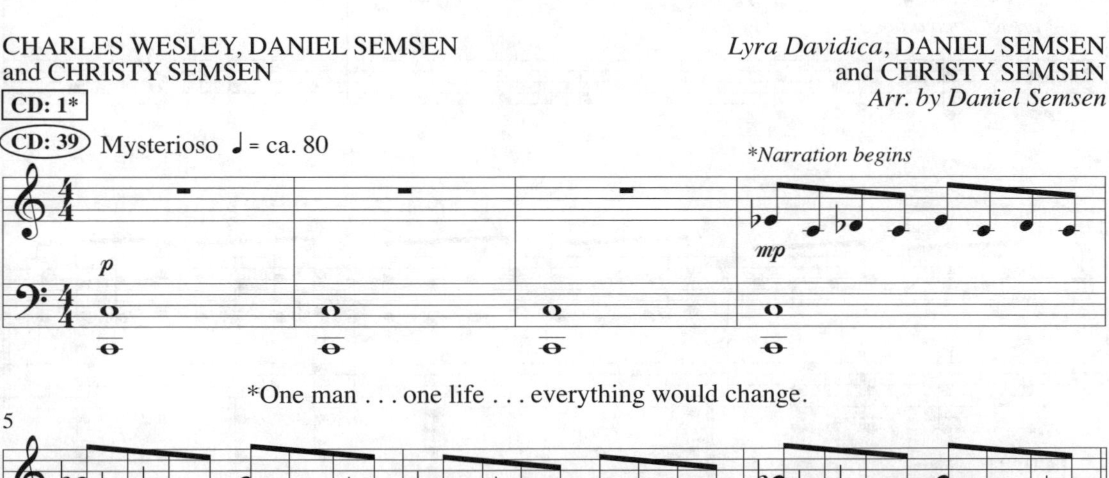

*One man . . . one life . . . everything would change.

**His arrival was noticed by wealthy and poor alike though
He would grow up in relative obscurity.

You may not have noticed Him had you passed Him on the street.
But He astounded the experts with His insight.

He grew in wisdom and stature.
He fed the poor . . . healed the sick . . . touched the untouchable . . .
taught the experts . . . noticed the outcasts . . . forgave the criminal . . .
One life turned the world upside-down.

*CD POINTS: Split-channel, CD:1-38; Stereo Trax, CD:39-76; Vocal Demo, CD:77-80

14

cresc. poco a poco

17

CD: 2

CD: 40 *Narration continues*

20

ff

*Betrayed by His own people . . . beaten and bruised . . .
sentenced as a common criminal . . . and falsely accused.
Finally killed in the most painful way imaginable . . .
He breathed His last breath . . . a breath of mercy for His killers.
And while the one life had mattered . . . it was finished . . .

CD: 3
CD: 41
*Narration continues
29
Am
F
f

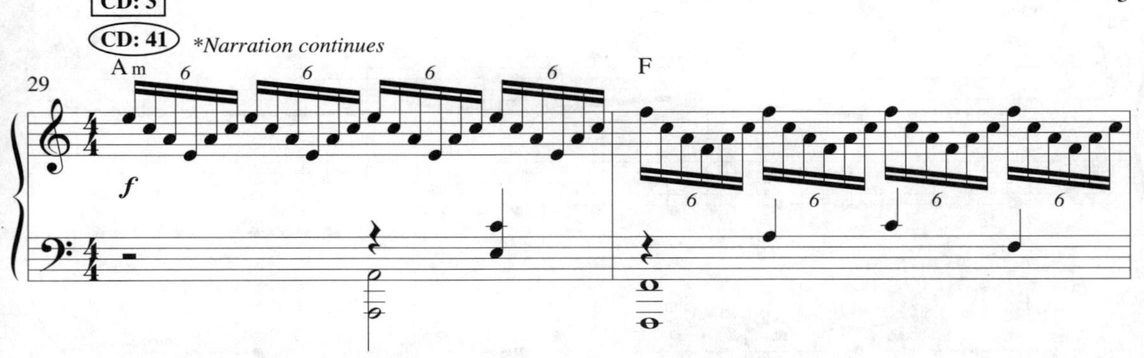

*BUT THEN on the third day . . .

Love pierced through the darkness and against all hope
the Savior of the World AROSE!
Crushing sin and death with glorious victory . . .
throwing back the curse of sin and conquering the grave.
Jesus the Christ had RISEN!

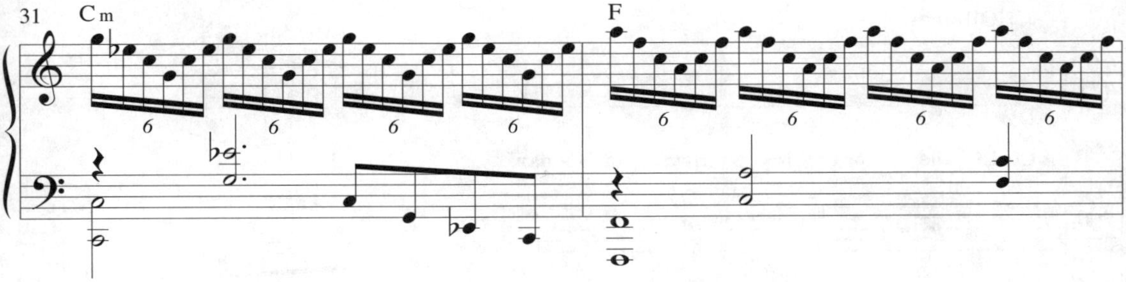

31
Cm
F

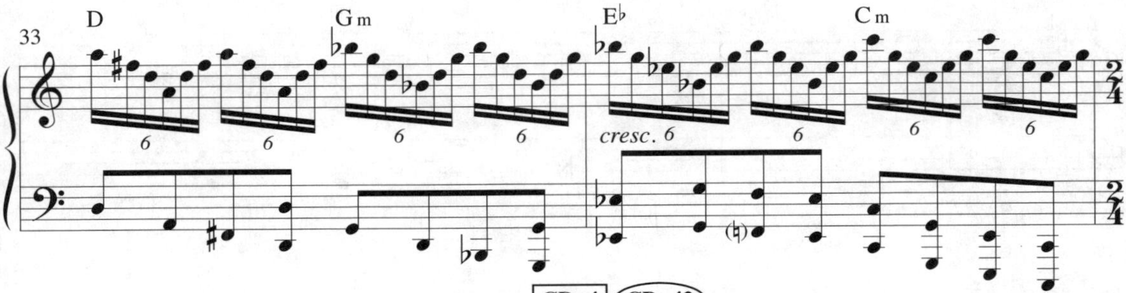

33
D
Gm
E♭
Cm
cresc.

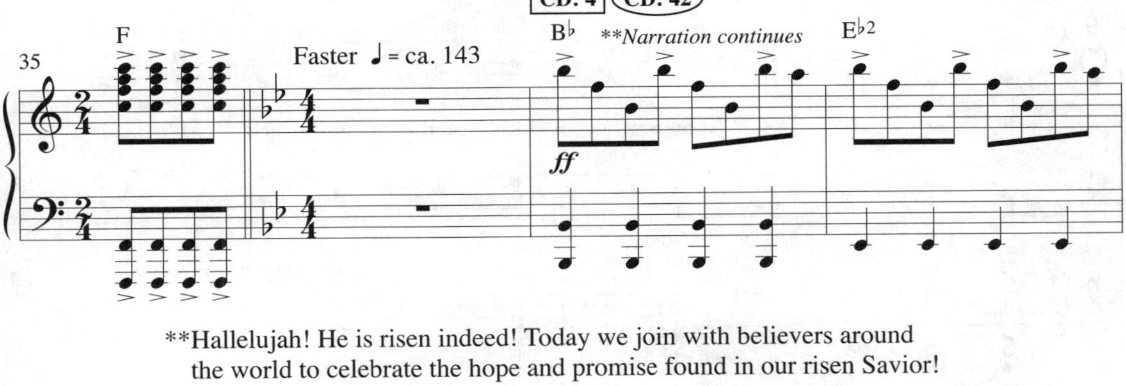

CD: 4
CD: 42
35
F
Faster ♩ = ca. 143
B♭
**Narration continues
E♭2
ff

**Hallelujah! He is risen indeed! Today we join with believers around
the world to celebrate the hope and promise found in our risen Savior!

Let's sing as one, praise the the Risen King!

39
Gm7
Fsus
F
B♭
42
E♭2
Gm7
Fsus
F
45
CHOIR unis.
mf
Christ the Lord is ris'n to - day.
Al - le -
mf
B♭
E♭
Gm7
E♭
mf
48
lu - ia!
Sons of men and an - gels say:
B♭/F
F
B♭
E♭
Cm7
F(no3)

51
Al - le - lu - ia! Raise your joys and
Gm7 E♭ B♭/F F B♭ F
54
tri - umphs high. Al - le - lu - ia!
B♭ F B♭ F/C C F
57
Sing, ye heav'ns, and earth, re - ply: Al - le -
F B♭ E♭ Gm7 E♭

CD: 5
CD: 43
60
mf
lu - ia!
Lives a - gain our
mf
B♭/F F B♭ B♭sus B♭
64
glo - rious King. Al - le - lu - ia!
E♭ Gm7 E♭ B♭/F F B♭
67
Where, O death, is now thy sting? Al - le -
E♭ Cm7 F(no3) Gm7 E♭

70
lu - ia! Dy - ing once, He all doth save.
Bb/F F Bb F Bb
73
Al - le - lu - ia! Where thy vic - to -
F Bb F/C C F Bb
CD: 6
CD: 44
76
cresc.
ry, O grave? Al - le - lu -
Eb Gm7 Eb Bb/F F

79
f
ia!
He a-rose,
shout and praise
B♭
F
82
Him,
al - le - lu - ia.
He a-rose,
E♭
B♭
85
the pow'r of sin is bro - ken
and we have been set free.
F
E♭
E♭m7
F

88
He a-rose, cre-a-tion's sing - ing al-le-lu-
F
E♭
91
- ia. He a-rose, the Son of God vic-tor-
B♭
F
94
mf
- ious and He reigns for-ev - er - more, Al-le-lu-
mf
E♭
G♭
F m7

CD: 7
CD: 45
97
- ia!
Love's re - deem - ing work is done.
B♭
B♭sus
B♭
E♭
mf
101
Al - le - lu - ia!
Fought the fight, the
Gm7
E♭
B♭/F
F
B♭
E♭
104
bat - tle won.
Al - le - lu - ia!
Cm7
F(no3)
Gm7
E♭
B♭/F
F
B♭

107
Death in vain for - bids Him rise. Al - le -
F
B♭
F
B♭
110
lu - ia! Christ has o - pened par - a - dise.
F/C
C
F
B♭
E♭
CD: 8
CD: 46
113
Al - le - lu - ia! He a - rose,
f
Gm7
E♭
B♭/F
F
B♭
f

116

shout and praise Him, al - le - lu - - ia.

F E♭ B♭

119

He a-rose, the pow'r of sin is bro - ken and

B♭ F E♭

125
ing al - le - lu - ia.
He a - rose,
E♭
B♭
128
the Son of God vic - tor - ious and He reigns for - ev - er - more,
F
E♭
G♭
Fm7
CD: 9
CD: 47
131
mp
Al - le - lu - ia!
LADIES unis.
He a - rose,
Fm7
B♭
mp

134
al - le - lu - ia, He a - rose.
It is done,
G♭
A♭
B♭
Ped.
8vb
CD: 10
CD: 48
138
sin is con - quered, He's a - live.
He a - rose,
Add MEN
mp
E♭m7
Fm7
B♭
8vb
142
al - le - lu - ia, He a - rose.
G♭
A♭
B♭

CD: 11
CD: 49
145
It is done, sin is con - quered, He's a - live.
B♭
E♭m7
Fm7
148
mf
He a - rose, al - le - lu -
mf
B♭
A♭
mf
151
- ia, He a - rose.
It is done,
B♭
C

154
sin is con - quered, He's a - live.
Fm7
Gm7
C
157
f
He a - rose,
al - le - lu - ia, He a - rose.
C
A♭
B♭
160
It is done,
sin is con -
C
Fm7

CD: 12

CD: 50

163

-quered, He's a-live. He a-rose,

Gm7 C

166

shout and praise Him, al-le-lu-ia.

G F C

mp

169

He a-rose, the pow'r of sin is bro-ken and

C G F

172
we have been set free.
He a-rose,
cre-a-tion's sing-
Fm7
G
175
-ing
al-le-lu-ia.
He a-rose,
F
C
178
the Son of God vic-tor-ious
and He reigns
for-ev-er-more,
G
F
A♭
Gm7

181

Yes, He reigns for - ev - er - more. Jesus

Gm7 A♭ Gm7

184

cresc.

reigns for - ev - er - more.

ff

Fm7 B♭ C

187

He a-rose.

(8)

F/C F C

8va

8vb

Jesus Is Alive

Words and Music by
DAVID MOFFITT, TRAVIS COTTRELL
and SUE C. SMITH
Arr. by Daniel Semsen

CD: 13
CD: 51
Driving rock ♩ = ca. 137

G (no3) F/G C/G

f

10
of the Son, "It is fin - ished."
C/G
G (no3)
Gm7
13
From the sky came the thun - der, the light - ning, the rain.
Gm7
C/G
15
In the tomb, hope was si -
G (no3)
Gm7
C/G

18

-lent and still___ in the dark - ness. Then

C/G G (no3)

21

CD: 14

CD: 52

up from the grave___ He a - rose!___

C D Em

23

cresc.

f

Up from the grave___ He a - rose!___ Hal - le - lu -

F2 C

25
- jah to the Sav - ior! Lamb cru - ci - fied, now
G
f
D
F2
28
glo - ri - fied! Hal - le - lu - jah, ris - en Re - deem - er!
C
G
Dm
31
We live to tes - ti - fy; Je - sus is a - live!
C2
F2
G (no 3)
F
G

CD: 15
CD: 53
34
F/G
C/G
Gm7
37
mf
Now the pow - er of sin and de-spair has been bro -
mf
Gm7
C/G
mf
39
- ken.
Now the dark - ness of death
G (no3)
Gm7
C/G

42
— is de-feat - ed at — last.
C/G
G (no3)
Gm7
45
We will live — in His pres - ence and praise — Him for - ev -
Gm7
C/G
47
- er,
'Cause up from the grave — He a-rose! —
G (no3)
C
D
Em

CD: 16
CD: 54
50
cresc.
f
Up from the grave He a-rose! Hal-le-lu-
cresc.
f
Em
F2
C
53
-jah to the Sav-ior! Lamb cru-ci-fied, now
G
D
F2
f
56
glo-ri-fied! Hal-le-lu-jah, ris-en Re-deem-er!
C
G
Dm

59
We live to tes - ti - fy;
Je - sus is a - live!
C2
F2
G (no3)
F
G
CD: 17
CD: 55
62
F
G
C
G
65
LADIES unis.
mp
He's a - live,
now the bat - tle's won!
He's a - live,
G (no3)
G sus
F2
G
sub. mp

68
now the curse is gone! He's a-live, tore the bars a - way!
C/G
G (no3)
G sus

CD: 18
71
CD: 56
He's a-live, it's a brand new day! He's a-live,
Add MEN
mf
He is a-live!
F2/G
C/G
G (no3)
mf

74
now the bat - tle's won! He's a-live, now the curse is gone!
He is a-live!
G sus
F2/G
C/G

CD: 19
CD: 57
77
He's a - live,
tore the bars a - way!
He's a - live,
He is a - live!
He is a - live!
G (no3)
G sus
F2/G
80
it's a brand new day!
He's a - live,
He is a - live!
f
C/G
A♭(no3)
82
now the bat - tle's won!
He's a - live,
now the curse is gone!
He is a - live!
A♭sus
G♭2/A♭
D♭/A♭

CD: 20
CD: 58
85
He's a-live,
tore the bars a - way!
He's a-live,
He is a-live!
He is a-live!
A♭(no3)
A♭sus
G♭2
A♭
88
it's a brand new day!
ff
He's a-live,
He is a-live!
D♭
A♭
A (no3)
90
now the bat - tle's won!
He's a-live,
He is a-live!
A sus
G2

92
now the curse is gone!
He's a - live,
He is a - live!
D/F♯
A/E
CD: 21
CD: 59
94
tore the bars a - way!
He's a - live!
f
Hal - le - lu -
A sus/D
G 2
97
- jah to the Sav - ior!
Lamb cru - ci - fied, now
A N.C.
(drums only)

100
glo - ri - fied! Hal - le - lu - jah, ris - en Re - deem -
CD: 22
CD: 60
102
- er! We live to tes - ti - fy! Hal - le - lu -
D2
G2
f
105
- jah to the Sav - ior! Lamb cru - ci - fied, now
A
E
G2

CD: 23

CD: 61

108

glo-ri-fied! Hal-le-lu - jah, ris-en Re-deem - er!

D A Em

111

We live to tes-ti-fy; Je-sus is a-live! We live to tes-ti-fy;

D2 G2 D2

114

ff

Je-sus is a-live! We live to tes-ti-fy; Je-sus is a-live!

ff

G2 D2 G2

117
Jesus is
A (no3)
A sus
G2/B
ff
120
a - live!
He's a - live!
D
A (no3)
A sus
123
molto rit.
(8)
He's a - live!
G2/B
D
A
(8)
8va
molto rit.
8vb

All to Us

Words and Music by
JESSE REEVES, CHRIS TOMLIN,
MATT REDMAN and MATT MAHER
Arr. by Daniel Semsen

CD: 24
CD: 62

Ballad feel ♩ = ca. 65

E♭ Gm Fsus F E♭ Gm

mp

4

LADIES *unis.*

p

Pre - cious Cor - ner-stone, sure foun -

Fsus F E♭ B♭/D

p

6

da - tion, You are faith - ful to the end; We are

F/A B♭ E♭ B♭/D Fsus F

9

wait - ing on You, Je - sus, We be - lieve You're all ___ to

E♭ B♭/D F/A Gm E♭ F

CD: 25

CD: 63

12

CHOIR *unis.*

mp

us.

Pre - cious

mp

E♭ Gm Fsus F

14

Cor - ner-stone, sure foun - da - tion, You are

E♭ B♭/D F/A B♭

mp

16
faith - ful to the end; We are wait - ing on You,
E♭
B♭/D
F sus
F
E♭
B♭/D
CD: 26
CD: 64
19
mf
Je - sus, We be - lieve You're all to us. Let the
mel.
mf
F/A
G m
E♭
F
B♭
22
glo - ry of Your name be the pas - sion of the Church; Let the
F
mf
E♭
B♭

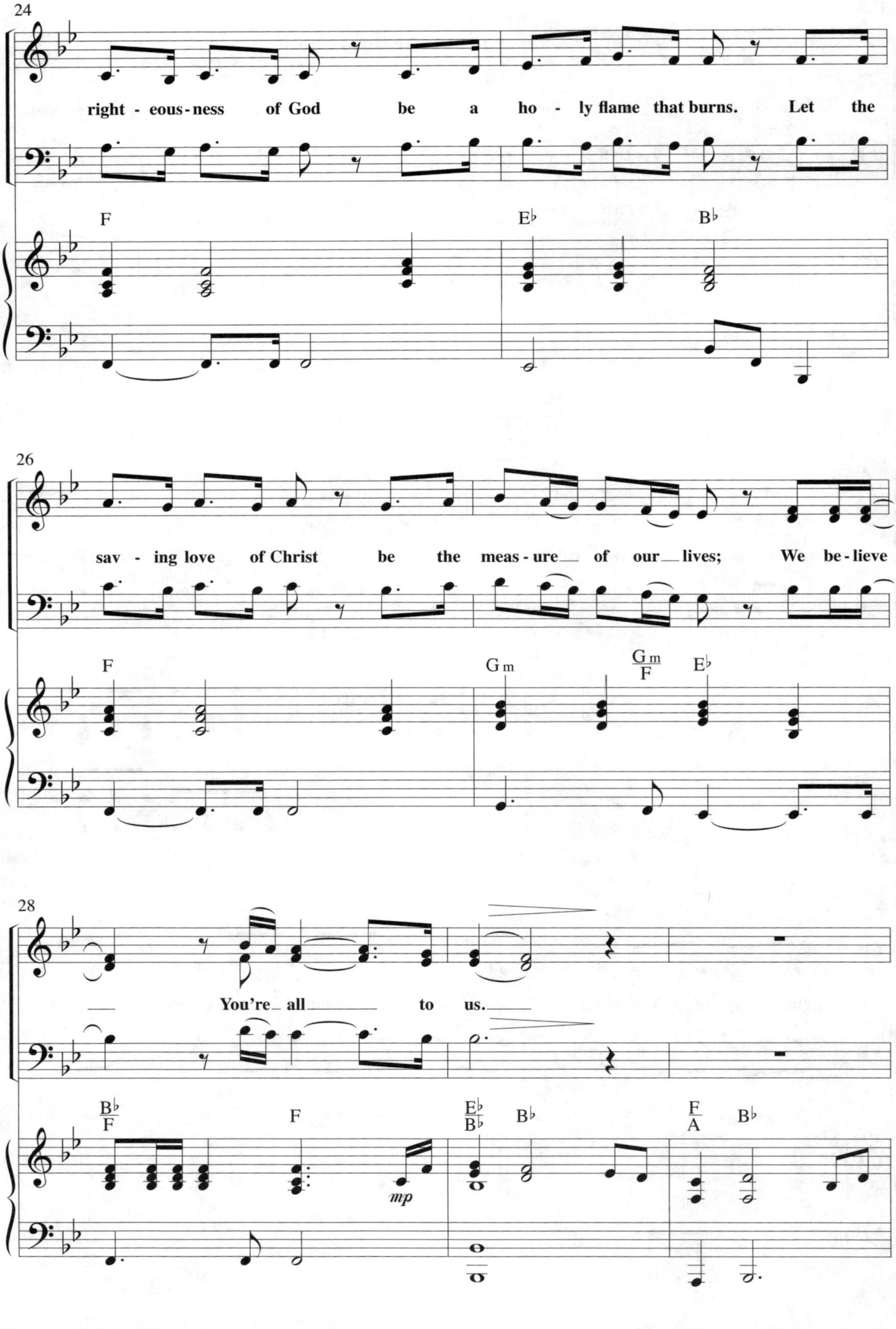

24

right - eous - ness of God be a ho - ly flame that burns. Let the

F E♭ B♭

26

sav - ing love of Christ be the meas - ure of our lives; We be - lieve

F Gm Gm/F E♭

CD: 27
CD: 65
31
mel. mf
On - ly Son of God sent from
mf
E♭
B♭/D
cresc.
F sus
F
mf
E♭
B♭
34
heav - en, Hope and mer - cy at the
F/A
B♭
E♭
B♭
36
cresc.
cross; You are ev - 'ry - thing, You're the
cresc.
F
E♭
B♭

CD: 28
CD: 66
38
prom - ise, Je - sus, You are all to
F/A Gm E♭ F
cresc.
40
f
us. Let the glo - ry of Your name be the
B♭ F F/A
42
pas - sion of the Church; Let the right - eous - ness of God be a
E♭/G B♭ F F/A

44
ho - ly flame that burns. Let the sav - ing love of Christ be the
E♭/G
B♭
F
F/A
CD: 29
CD: 67
46
meas - ure of our lives; We be - lieve You're all to
Gm
F
E♭
B♭/F
F
48
us. Let the glo - ry of Your name be the
B♭
F
F/A

50
pas - sion of the Church; Let the right - eous - ness of God be a
Eb/G
Bb
F
F/A
52
ho - ly flame that burns. Let the sav - ing love of Christ be the
Eb/G
Bb
F
F/A
54
meas - ure of our lives; We be - lieve You're all to
Gm
F
Eb
Bb/F
F

CD: 30

CD: 68

56

ff

us.

You're

ff

B♭

cresc.

58

all ___ to ___ us. You're all ___ to ___

E♭ Gm F B♭ E♭ Gm

ff

61

us. You're all ___ to ___

F/A B♭ E♭ Gm

CD: 31
CD: 69
63
Yes, You are.
Yes, You are.
us.
Yes, You are.
Yes, You are.
Yes, You are.
You are, You are.
Cm
E♭
F
B♭
65
You're
all
to
us.
You're
F
A
B♭
E♭
Gm
F
B♭
68
all
to
us.
You're
E♭
Gm
F
A
B♭

70

all to us You are.

C m7 B♭/D C m/E♭ F

8vb

CD: 32

CD: 70

72

slight rit. *p* *a tempo*

When this pass - ing world is

p

B♭ E♭ B♭/D

mf dim. *slight rit.* *p a tempo*

75

rit. poco a poco to end

o - ver, We will see You face to face; And for -

F/A B♭ E♭ B♭/D F/A

rit. poco a poco to end

(Without music)

NARRATOR: On this day of celebration and remembrance,
we humbly bow our hearts before the One who is everything to us.

(Music begins)

One life, whose ultimate sacrifice would alter humanity's future.
One life, who turned the world upside-down.
And now, this one life not only has changed eternity,
but changes hearts and lives today.

Jesus Saves

Words and Music by
TRAVIS COTTRELL
and DAVID MOFFITT
Arr. by Daniel Semsen

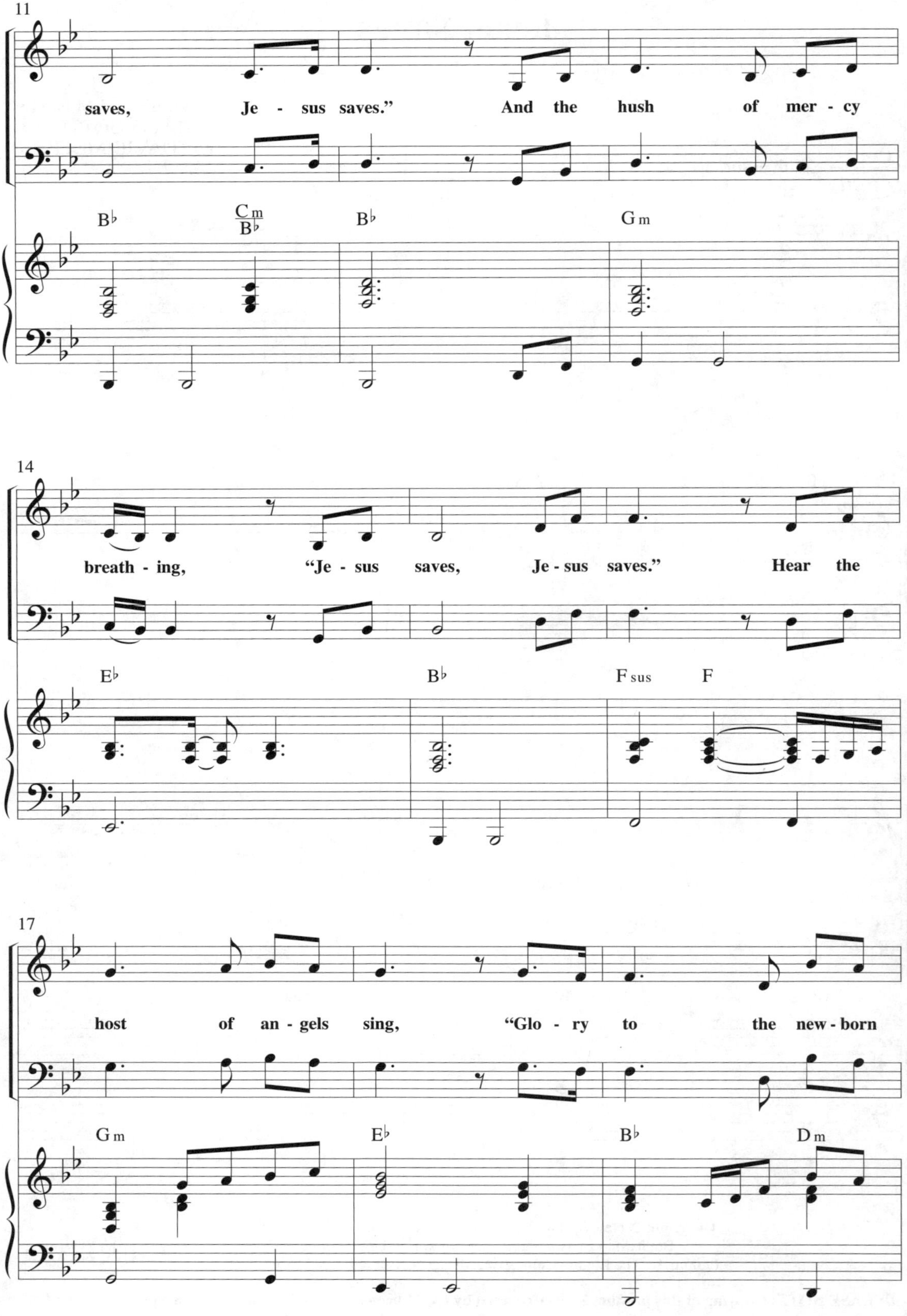

11

saves, Je - sus saves." And the hush of mer - cy

B♭ Cm/B♭ B♭ Gm

14

breath - ing, "Je - sus saves, Je - sus saves." Hear the

E♭ B♭ Fsus F

CD: 34
CD: 72
20
King." And the sound - ing joy re - peat - ing, "Je - sus
E♭
B♭/F
D m
E♭
23
mf
saves." See the hum - blest hearts a -
mf
B♭
B♭sus
B♭
cresc.
mf
26
dore Him. Je - sus saves, Je - sus saves. And the
B♭sus
B♭
C m/B♭
B♭

29
wis - est bow be - fore Him. Je - sus saves, Je - sus
Gm
E♭
B♭

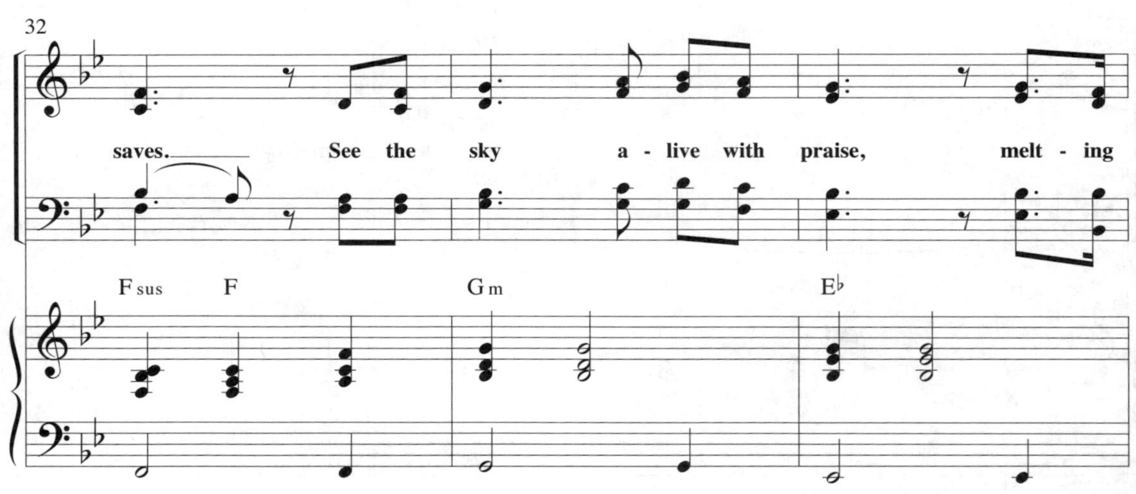
32
saves. See the sky a - live with praise, melt - ing
Fsus
F
Gm
E♭

35
dark - ness in its blaze. There is light for - ev - er -
B♭
Dm
E♭
B♭/F
Dm

CD: 35
CD: 73
38
dim.
p
more in "Je - sus saves." He will
dim.
p
E♭
B♭
B♭sus
B♭
dim.
41
live our sor - row shar - ing. Je - sus
B♭
B♭sus
p
43
saves, Je - sus saves. He will
B♭
Cm
B♭
B♭

45
die our bur - den bear - ing. Je - sus
Gm
E♭
47
cresc.
saves, Je - sus saves. "It is
cresc.
B♭
F sus
F
cresc.
49
f
mel.
done!" will shout the cross, "Christ has paid re - demp - tion's
f
Gm
E♭
B♭
Dm
f

CD: 36
CD: 74
52
mel.
cost." While the emp - ty tomb's de - clar - ing, "Je - sus
E♭
B♭/F
D m
E♭
55
saves!"
Free - dom's call - ing, chains are
B♭
B♭sus
B♭
F/A
G m
58
fall - ing, hope is dawn - ing bright and true.
Day is
E♭
B♭
F
F sus

61
breaking, night is quaking. God is making all things
Gm
E♭
B♭
CD: 37
CD: 75
64
cresc.
rit.
ff
new. Jesus saves! O to
F
Fsus
E♭
F/E♭
E♭M7
E♭/F
67
a tempo
grace, how great a debtor, Jesus saves, Jesus
C
Csus
Dm/C
ff a tempo

70
saves. Are the saints who shout to - geth - er, Je - sus
C
Am
F
73
saves, Je - sus saves. Ris - ing up so vast and
C
Gsus
G
Am
CD: 38
CD: 76
76
strong, lift - ing up sal - va - tion's song! The re -
F
C
C
E
F

79
Je - sus
deemed will sing
for - ev - er,
for - ev - er, sing for - ev - er,
C/G Em F F/A

82
saves!
Je - sus
Je - sus saves! Je - sus saves!
Je - sus saves!
Je - sus
Je - sus saves!
C C/E F

85
saves!
Je - sus
saves!
Je - sus
saves!
Je - sus
saves!
Je - sus
saves!
Je - sus
saves!
Je - sus
F/A
F
C
C/E

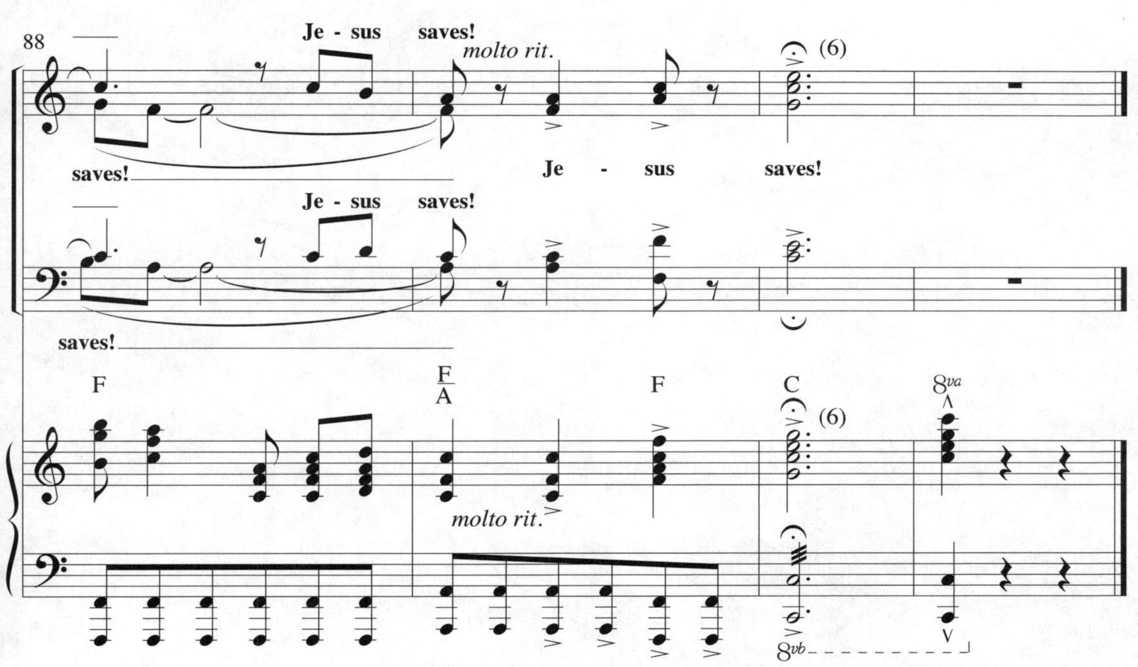
88
Je - sus
saves!
molto rit.
(6)
saves!
Je - sus
saves!
Je - sus
saves!
saves!
F
F/A
F
C
8va
(6)
molto rit.
8vb